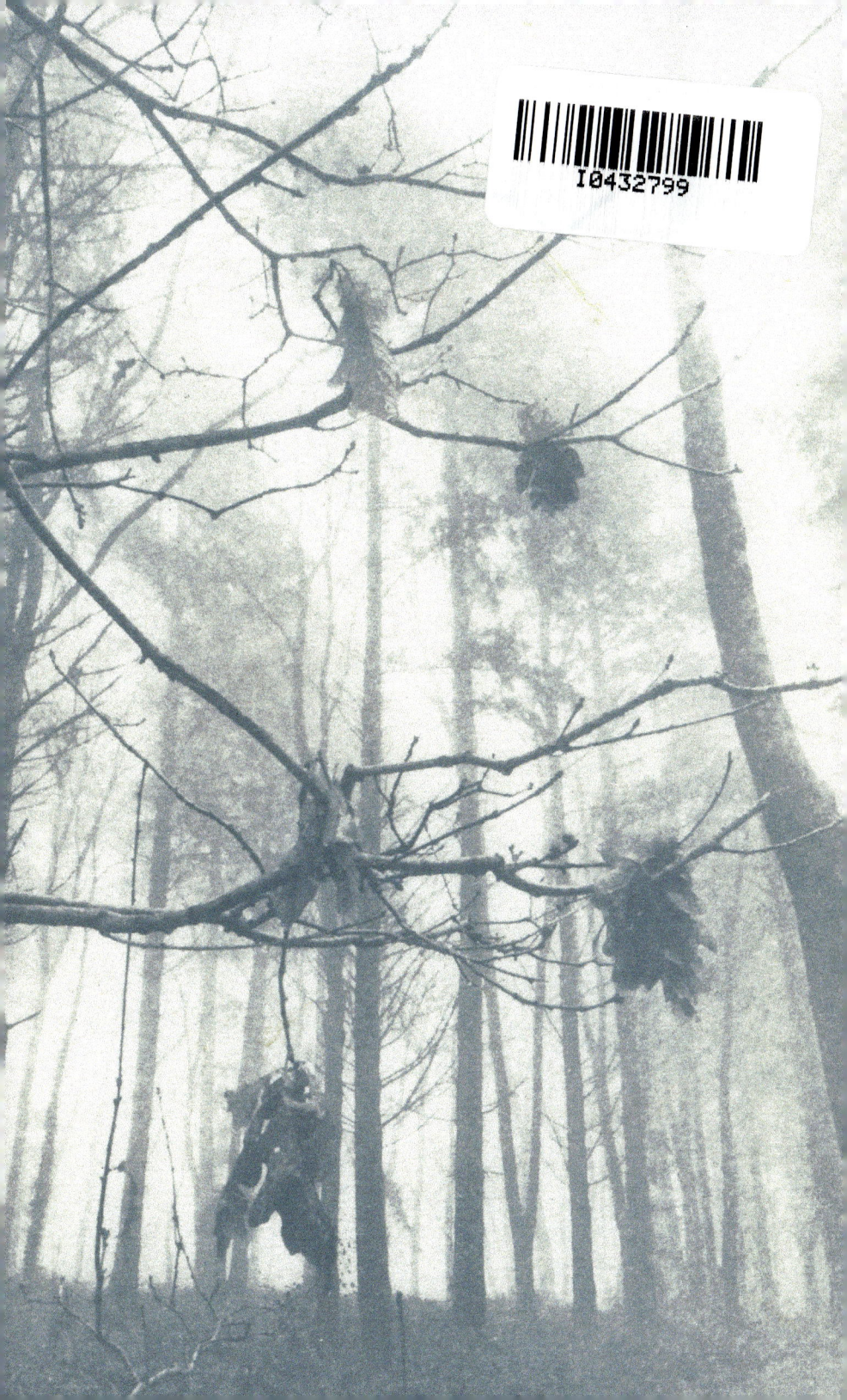

SOMEWHERE, LOOKING

Rollinson

© 2022 Amber Rollinson. All rights reserved; no part of this book may be reproduced by any means without the publisher's permission.

ISBN: 978-1-915079-26-8

The author has asserted their right to be identified as the author of this Work in accordance with the Copyright, Designs and Patents Act 1988

Cover image by Amber Rollinson

Cover designed by Aaron Kent

Edited and typeset by Aaron Kent

Broken Sleep Books Ltd
Rhydwen,
Talgarreg,
SA44 4HB
Wales

Contents

The Creek	9
Barn Owl	10
Spoon	11
The Seals	13
Cyanotype	14
The Escape	15
Somewhere, Looking	17
Archaeology	18
Conversations	19
Founder	21
Fear	25
Fernweh / Far Pain	26
The Old Canal	29
Deadwood	30
Seagrass Survey	31
Algal Bloom	33
Litho	34
Rain On the Map	37
Skerry	38
Acknowledgements	39

Somewhere, Looking

Amber Rollinson

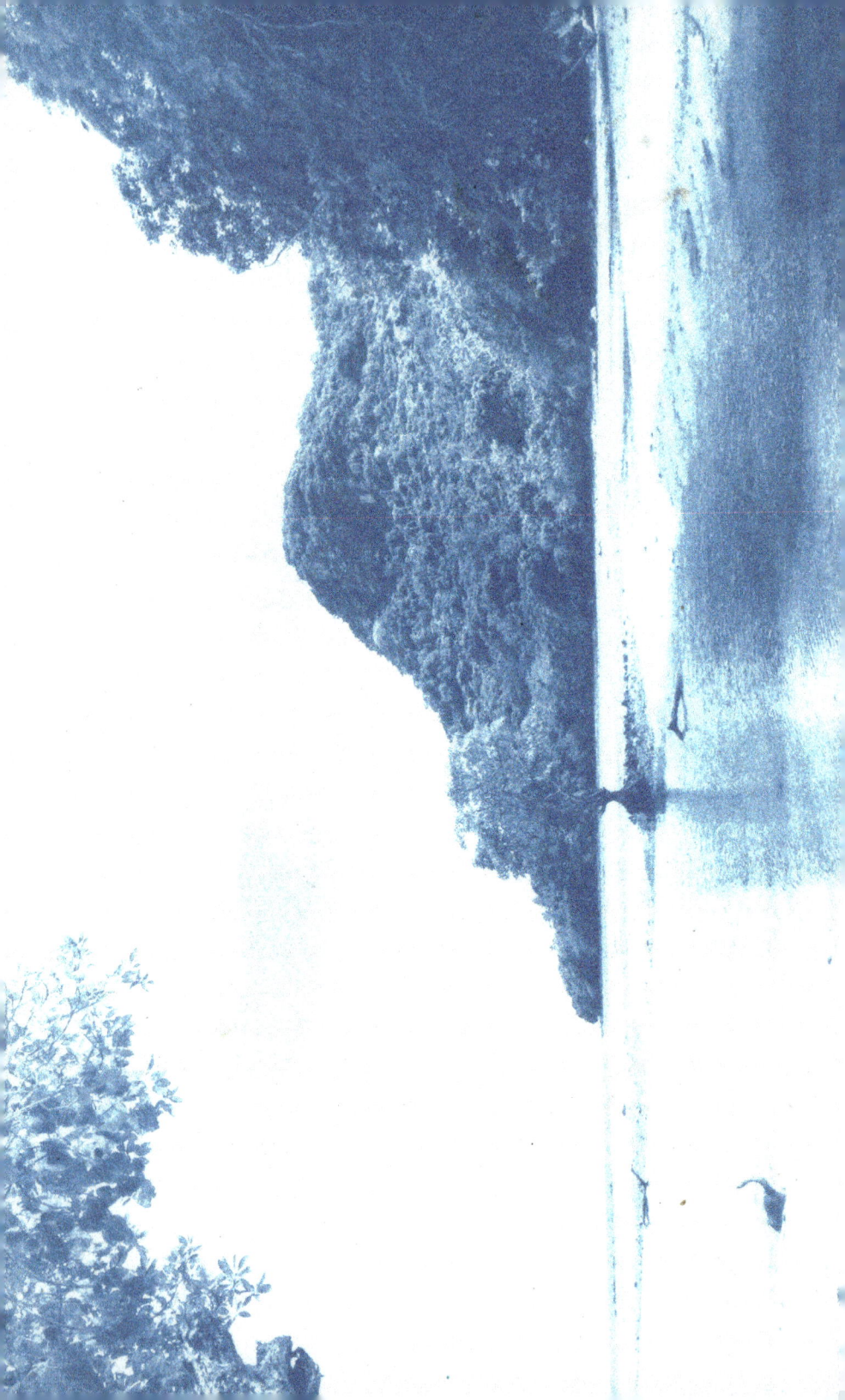

The Creek

he leans over, littoral-voiced, says
encounters change you

the sea converses with the land
breaks frail chunks

slithers up the creek, unwanted
mirrors sky

literally, erodes rock pits to gullies
before my eyes

he leans over, proud of his work
names birds

as if by magic
lingers over mangrove propagules

in severed bottles, misted plastic
neither one thing

nor the other, sea wears as some words do
encounters

change you, I don't remember
what he said next

something literal, but those
words broke off

taken by the sea

18.3828° S, 178.1194° E

Barn Owl

the moon is bright tonight
feathered ring of bronze
surrounding

cuts through darkness, thick, disturbs
no leaf, or strand of grass
unseen

sight is nothing, sounds cease mattering
but something surfaces where
nothing used to be

was it like the weight of occupied air
or conversation paused
solid?

the moon does not rest tonight
detaches raptorial
hover

from below they are fog curls, cloud cover
we cannot measure them
see instead

half-familiar faces
remembered from our dreams

Long Lane, near Felton Common

Spoon

It takes a while, but
he splits wood and strips away bark
from the pale interior

smells the oil
brings from the zip-pocket of his rucksack
a knife with a hooked end, whittles

moment by moment
the soft shape of a curved spoon.

The October sun is splintering
and all I hear is the *scrape scrape*
of blade

as embers from the fire hiss
he leans towards me, proud of his work

uses the thing he has made to scoop out
my eyes and eat them

leaving nothing behind

West Woods

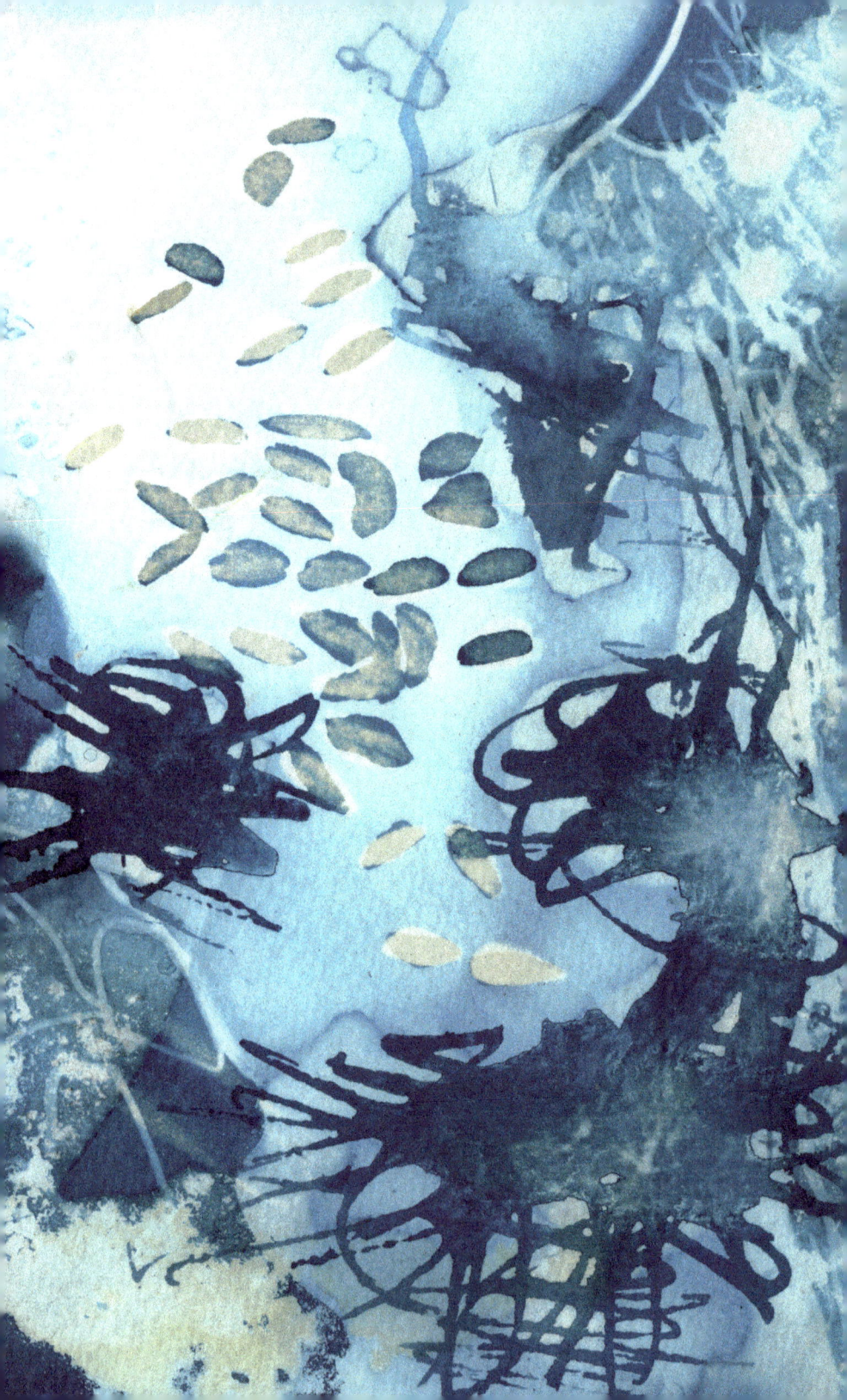

The Seals

I don't know why only the females have speckles

we speak in whispers as they settle
like thrown stones

the sun's gold on the sandbar, seal-flecked
curved like a neck, with netted throats

disturbed by speaking, they're like us, blue-fettered
slick but soft, he says. Inscrutable as rocks.

The wind serrates the headland, weather-punctured
we don't talk about the view

the slate-layered paths, like pages
folded to come back to

frayed shore and frail ledges
this wind-swept Atlantic coast shudders its broken edges

Just off B3301, North of Gwithian village

Cyanotype

I try bleaching the sun
using liquid soda crystals
but the sky turns yellow too,
wet paper lets it bleed

everything turns yellow
paper wears to holes –
that layer between image
and air so thin.

Is this how sunrise works?

I put tea leaves in a bucket
tone the sea until it glints
pollution brown, trap the sun
like a wasp in a glass
shifting across the paper.

Still, that disobedient buzzing sound.

The bathroom

The Escape

The carpet appears
gunmetal grey, like someone's
raked their hands over
the estuary, out here
walking from your mind

Grey rocks seem carpet
gaps in the hedge like windows
the single file track
with all the necessities
obvious to you, packed

The fact that water
becomes sea here and river
the other way, where
the line falls seems important
someone dragged who clung on

The pigeon above
cocks a head at you, looking
the silt tongue of her
as you follow the river
away from home, to the sea

But the mouth opens
baring algae-filmed teeth
and on the jetty ahead
a pebbledash house
it's yours, the pigeon lands

bladderwrack weaves rugs
as you open the door

Pigeon House Bay

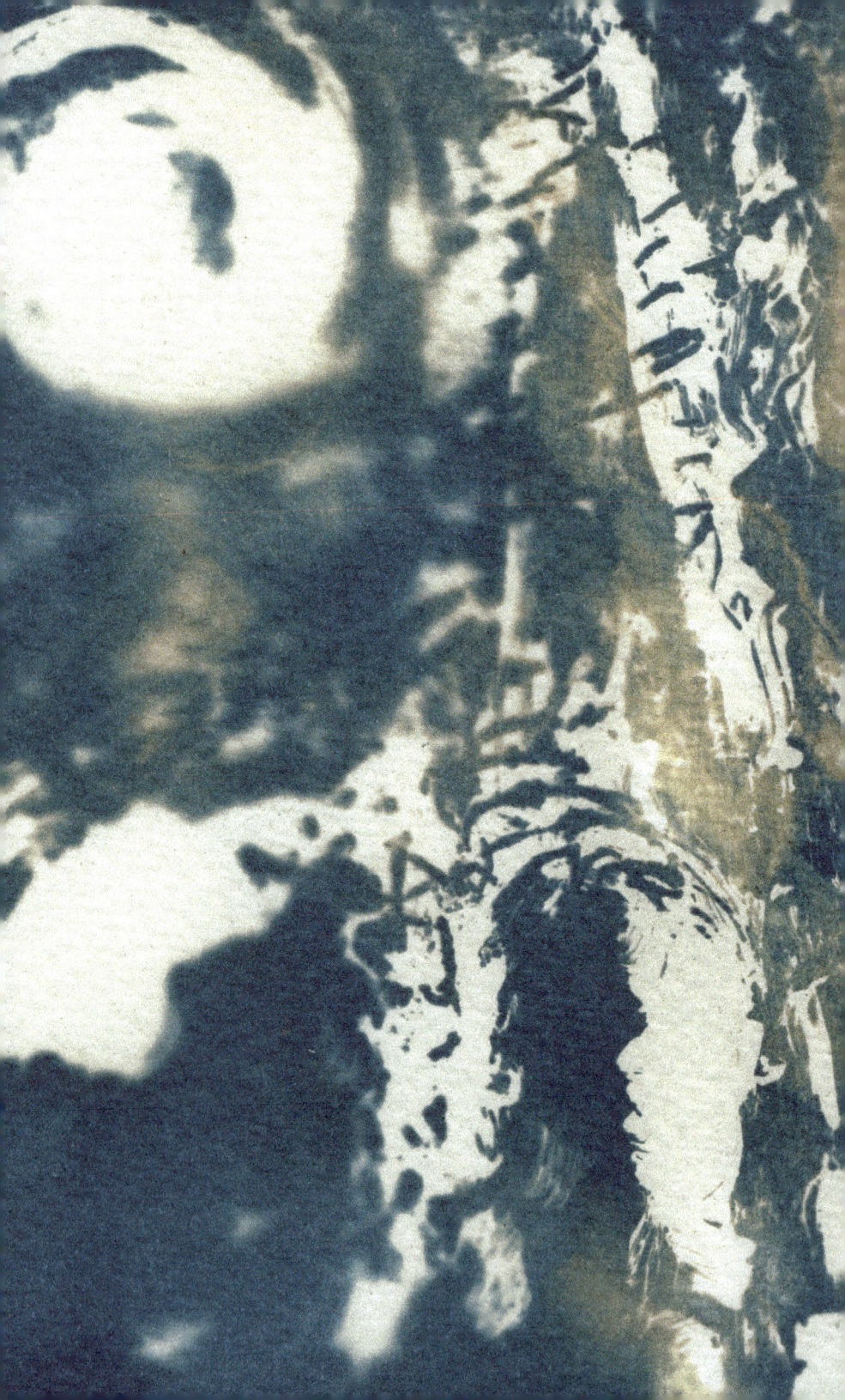

Somewhere, Looking

on this beach night settles
there are black streaks on the sand

coat pockets clack with rocks
throwing stones and shells

around you wick things like candlewicks
reaching ends, their end of story
pale moths

you came here to occupy yourself
now search for driftwood, smoothed to bone

they do not expect to reach the moon
so burn, only knowing where to go
from before

this might have fallen in, you say
up the estuary, near breeding eels
and flown

clear when young, and like glass
see through, but seeing you

looking up, the moon paints the sea white
cratered, pinned moth to the sky

somewhere on the dark sand
something you dropped

the back of your neck aches
skeletally

you stoop low

SW 5780 4138

Archaeology

There's the millpond, one of only
waterlogged sites nationally to retain
metal-detecting at dawn before
they wake up, the people who live there now

watching me part soil with spade
metallic remains retaining the structure
I want to see sixteenth century
situating in corn-stubble
myself in claggy earth who names me

The canal took the powder back to the battles
I have designs on those battles, smoke
sweeping concentration of cries

I hear canons when I sleep, something
passed, limestone sediment
in the fields where I have to stay
faces appearing, who threaten me off
off – off

wake up, see me, crouched among crows
on dark fields stark
mineral, clear

John love, he's by the barns.

Coins from someone's pocket, up to me
caught searching for signs

The chase and the return, no slip
to read waterlogs of wet pages

unloved pages
drying in my hands.

The cornfield just off the main road

Conversations

After the island I came to another.
Herons on the shore   against.
I roam the streets to outpace the feeling
black & blue, trapped there   of tidal mud and empty creeks

the no one speaking   everything moving
the tarp that was blue too.

From my window over metal rooftops rusting, it is there
Telephone altarpiece   something I couldn't do
A wooden post which knits   overlapping
electrical maps of the world.

I've always enjoyed continuous sounds: the hiss of the shore
storms and electrical humming sounds that repeat
the provisional surface   insulator and
sources of interference   earth.

It was never easy   the weather in the going still
translating electrics into   knocked down and built again
when things were settled the whole place seemed brighter
neatly trimmed just a   wire loops hung like goals.
The gap didn't seem as long   and then I left the island.

18.3828° S, 178.1194° E

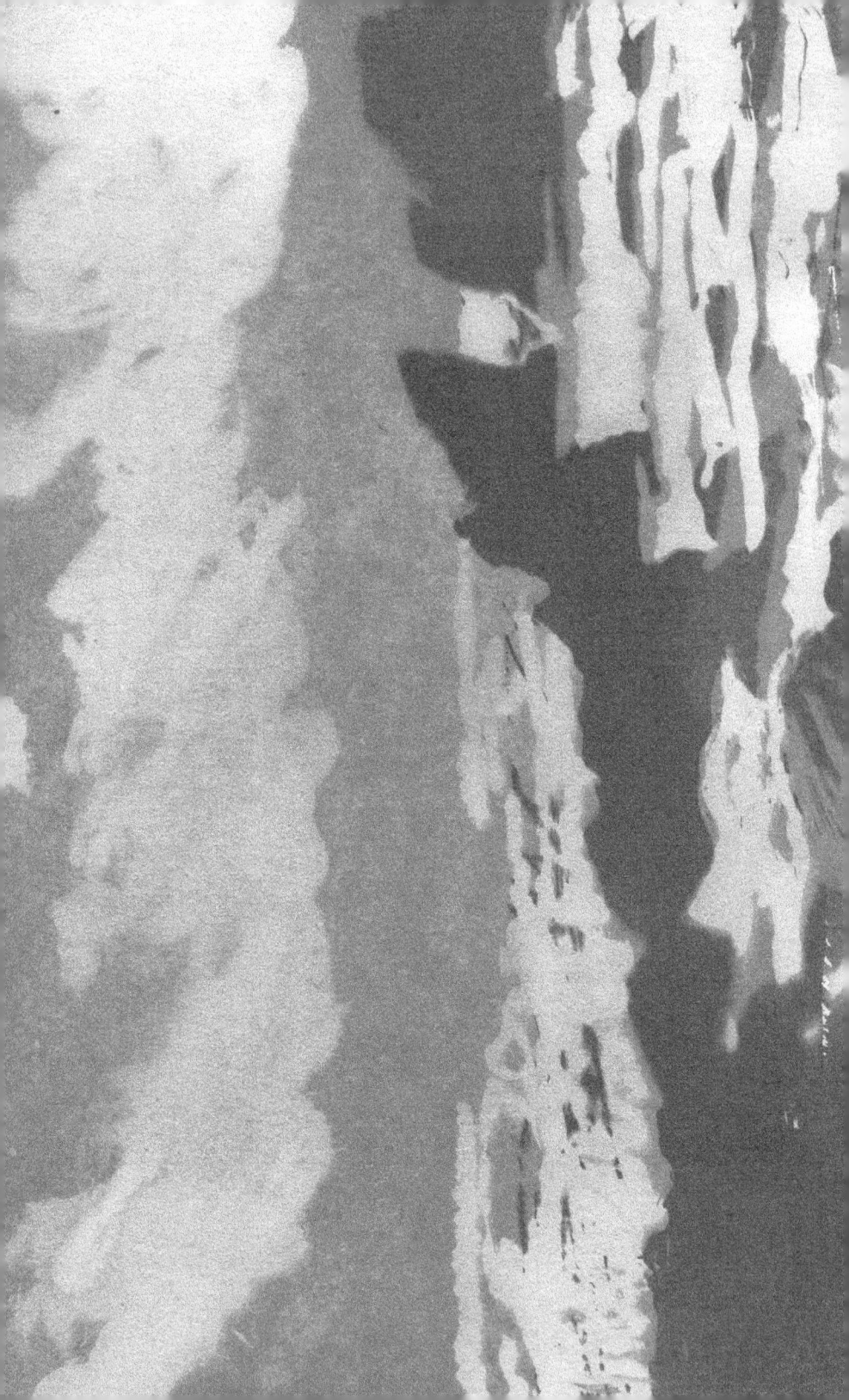

Founder

I

Rocks and white foam, salt air
scent of gorse flowers, coconut, gift

shops closed, dust-filmed done for
it's not the season.

This monochrome coast
this snake rock crumbling cliff-edge this

volcanic sand streaked black
this sea here

Skeleton grey gorse spines
with yellow faces, here we are

we're nowhere, slipping on rocks
furred-green

it's not the season.

II

The footpath has foundered
but we climb down anyway

he says it's like a washing machine
with too much powder, as wind lifts wisps of scum

The sea is a set of old curtains billowing
laundry left to dry

Sand not black as it seemed
from a distance – now I'm here – black

and white and red, the red and white additions like secrets
only the initiated know

What's that in the distance? A container ship, he says
Funny: it seemed an abandoned church

III

This monochrome coast, it talks, it's having conversations
but we don't

conversely, we look and climb rocks
that flake away to wet cliff shards in our hands

This falling rain, not like rain but powder, icing sugar
not black exactly but blue green, not

roaring especially, but wearing
wearing

Kynance Cove, Cornwall, UK

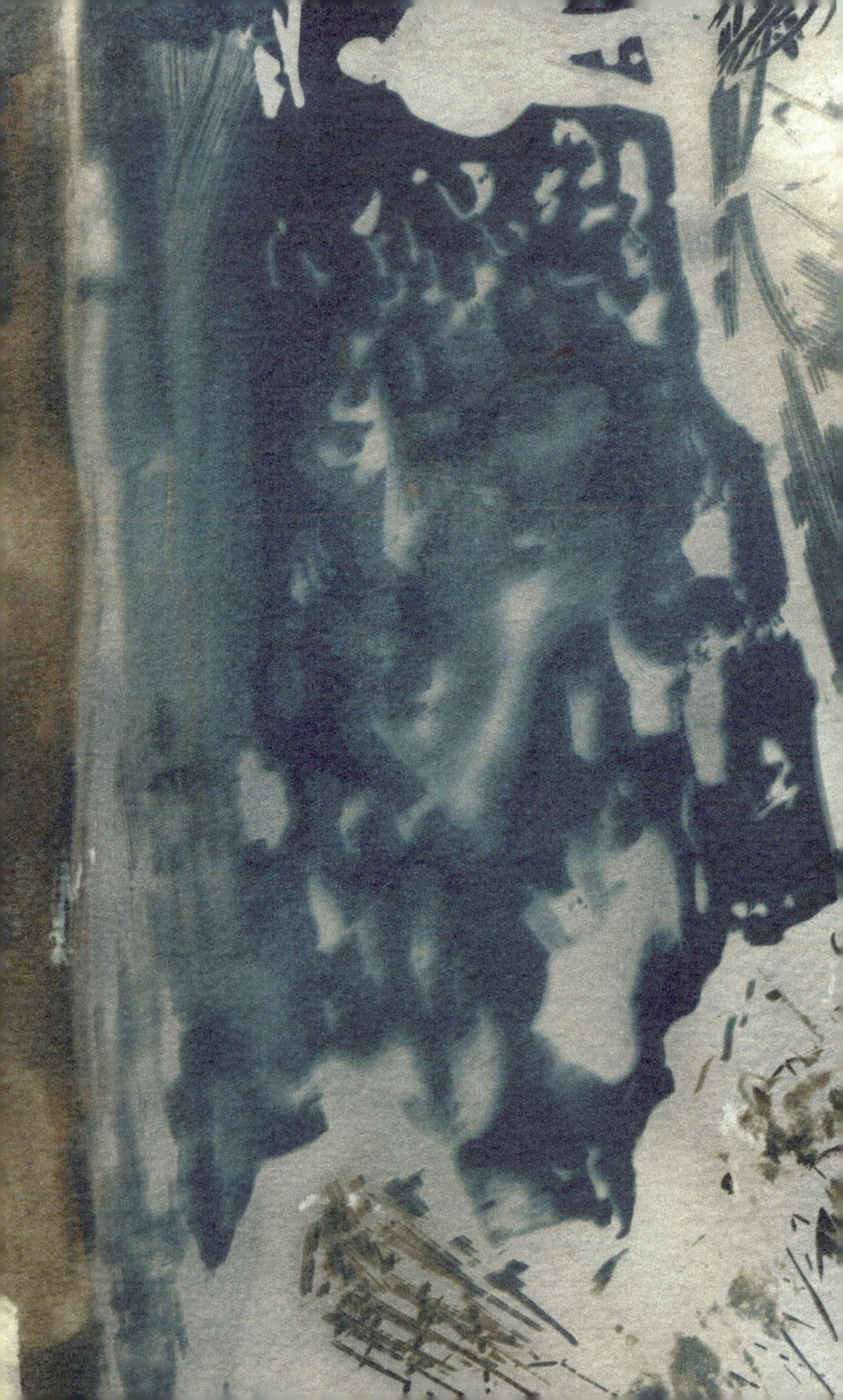

Fear

The glacier cracks
unfreezing with tears of meltwater

He turns out the light and leaves the room

>In the valley
>nets of mist catch strange moths
>out of context, allowed out
>a window, haunting empty streets

The glacier breathes, shuddering to gather snow
around her, becoming a woman.

Around her, becoming a woman
the glacier breathes, shuddering to gather snow

>a window, haunting empty streets
>out of context, allowed out
>nets of mist catch strange moths
>in the valley

He turns out the light and leaves the room

unfreezing with tears of meltwater
the glacier cracks

Anywhere

Fernweh / Far Pain

What is it but a scar of rock
a scab of green
and then a lighthouse?

I can't hear what they're saying
people I know and people I don't

grass sewn into verge by storm, a reminder
to keep

that certain quality of light here,
drawing artists who kept the light for others

wind that doesn't take my breath away, but
breathes into my mouth

some other

words of conversation, images
shudder the hood, carry the coast to my face

storm of skies, clashing heads
blurred words spoken by uneasy mouths

we are homesick for a place we haven't seen, lonely
for a love we've never known

looking for the lighthouse
gull-guarded scar

that glimmer written of light on water

remembered by others like thoughts turned on and off
projected

past rocks, who witness
out at sea

their slow mineral lives
and our own unhoming

Godrevy, Cornwall, UK

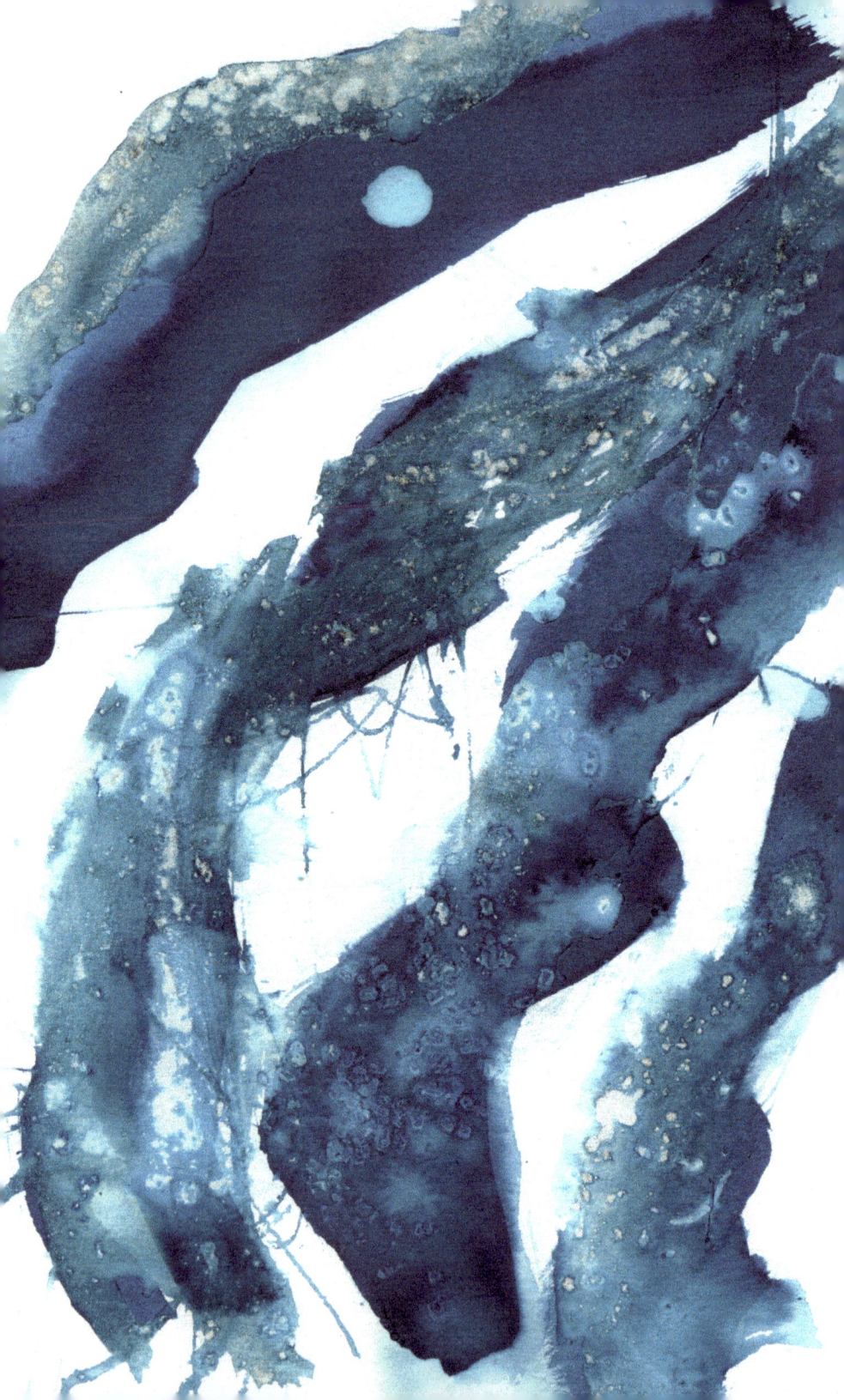

The Old Canal

under the river
rocks fur lurid green

    if there is a skin to water
    water must have flesh

sunlight writes white on the surface, marks
shadow-suns, blinding as some thoughts can be

    crowded alders needle sharp among the nests
    of pigeons, fat, with purple chests

there's a shadow of a person in the shadow
of this river

    ripple folds beneath another, folded leather
        turning over

white is cast like bleach
on ink, that yellow spray

    a cloud of midges hangs above, river frantic
    with bronze flies

the shadow surfaces, quivers grey

    the fleck of a minnow
    slipping away

51.3814° N, 2.6619° W

Deadwood

The forest swallows you, not
needing you

unable to resist, as looping round
you think of help

for you or this place's languid
yellow stream

the fern uncurls
tickling the roof of your mouth

behind grit-filmed teeth
veined by roots

you'd call if anyone was there
shade dappled creature that you are

the trunks thrum with water
amongst new life without you

but being born

Mendip Hills Area of Outstanding Natural Beauty

Seagrass Survey

the seagrass off the jetty
in leather ribbons, stubble, kneel
combing with dive slates suddenly there's
a scalding hollow at my knee feeling
rising to hips, bone-deep, I cry out
of jellyfish imprint, stingers clinging, climb to air
nettles stung the same, quavered with no core
all water, nearly, half-physical *fluther*
smuck on the beach, an immortal kiss
this wafting thing that thrives in dead zones
blankets fish-farms in plasticky sheets
formerly Medusa, form merely a flow from
body to mane, and mainly water they drift
near passive, but use the sun as compass
landmarks above water, wavering bodied
flowing from estuaries to wider sea
half-delirious, I howl while she emerges
to brush the stingers loose, pour vinegar
on the written-in-purple scar, half
resembling a noose

The north island

Algal Bloom

What's the point of a river
he says, flinging out his line
a green tongue grows thick
as things tend to grow, given
what they need above the banks
barns stacked with chickens
blinking, in the shallows
not even the smallest of creatures

His rod hangs empty, barren in hands
hook-cut as the dense carpet thickens
on the other bank, the heron still
that indistinct grey
of rainclouds half-way
between storm and vanishing

The river Wye

Litho

This is our first landfall after a
slow, intermittently
rocks fall below us – into flight

She is telling me about it as we walk the coast path

some people use aluminium, but I prefer the – harder to source mind but there you go – it's the knowledge isn't it, all that life written down?

The past ecology of her face
the spine of this folding
Spine of my
Wide range of marks and all of a

we take flight again.

She always knew how to use the hammer setting on the drill without flinching and when to cheer during a rugby match.

It's a matter of guess work
slow movements, riding airwaves, resting on a fence post,
softened by rain

A hovering kestrel, watching the seethe of the churn of the
See here, if I was an animal, you know, I'd be a bird.

The political question, she says. *What stands to be lost?*

First landfall we have
unconformity, serrated marram edges of the
come to infiltrate the folded chalk

Grey birds wheel over the estuary bottles
a rich discovery ground for fossils
that seam of grey tumbling out and
stirring things up.

Yes, it could form the basis of my next
We have to be off, and so we take

the story in the thick spine of her like a feather

The path to the Golden Cap

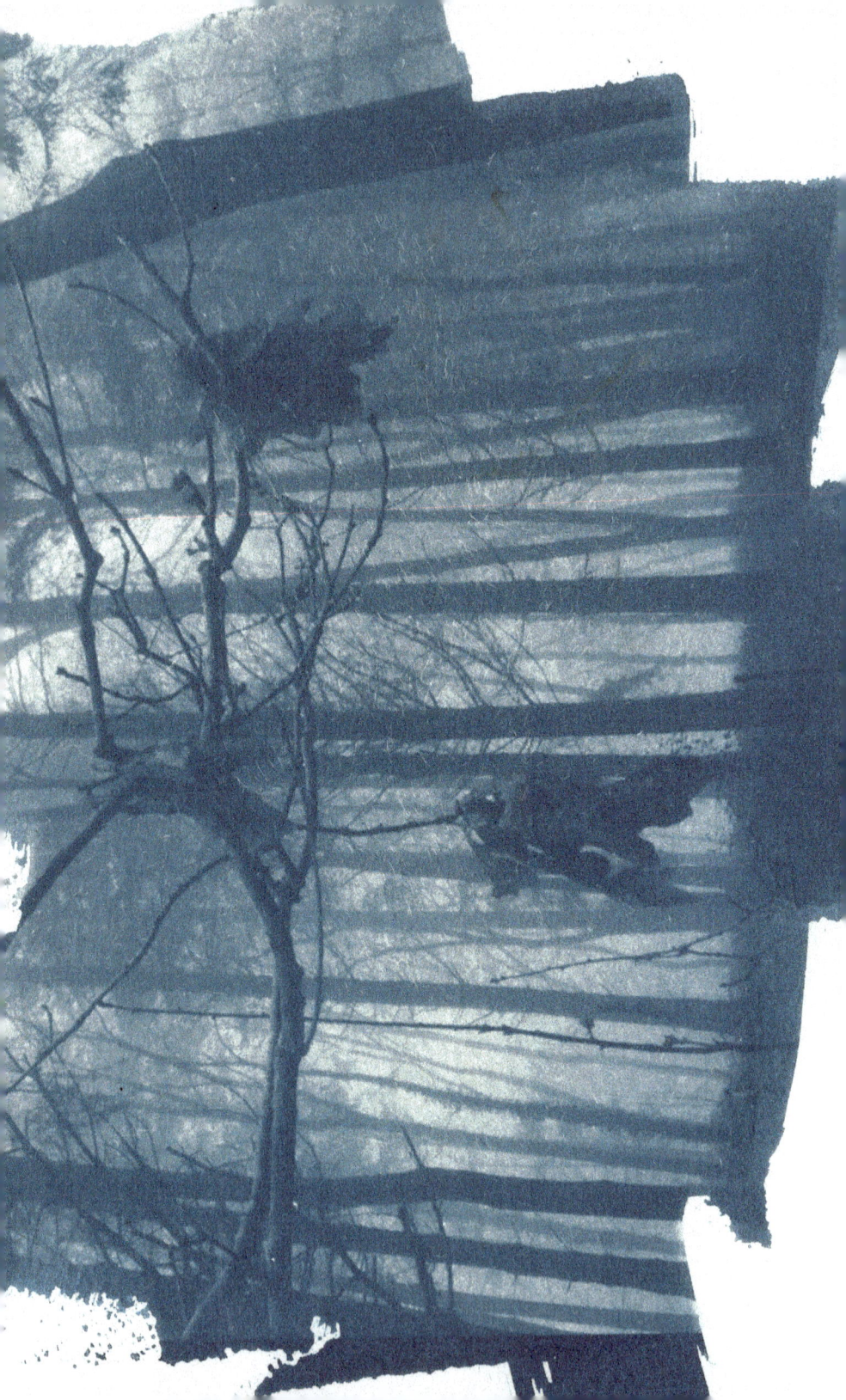

Rain On the Map

There are things I don't understand
        where rivers become sea, drawing that line
the way rain bends maps
        sometimes the path swells
unruly, mud-thick puddles
        hovering flies
tree trunks creak as they tighten
        rain falling, making the forest small
we edge around stagnant puddles
        falling in every time

        Falling in every time
we edge around stagnant puddles
        rain falling, making the forest small
tree trunks creak as they tighten
        hovering flies
unruly mud-thick puddles
        sometimes the path swells
the way rain bends maps
        where rivers become sea, drawing that line
there are things I don't understand

14 minutes via BS3130

Skerry

Out at sea, there is a rock
wet-edged, salt-polished, black

surf tumbles him, refines the form
prompts a thought I overhear

But sight is like a tether
to marram serrated shores

this edgeland of elements
becoming less, or more

a dark tooth, gull-haunted, lost
jaggedly out at sea, the rock

always where I am not

SW 6848 1303

Acknowledgements

Thank you to *époque press*, *Pulp Poets Press*, *Porridge*, *The Common Breath*, and *Channel Magazine* where versions of these poems first appeared. Thanks also to *Neon Magazine*, *Streetcake*, *Quince*, and *The Hopper* for publishing some of my cyanotypes.

I am forever grateful to the MSt Creative Writing at Oxford where I discovered my love for writing poetry, in particular to Jane Draycott whose first assignment resulted in 'Conversations', and Helen Mort who supervised my first year project.

Finally, thank you to Martyn Grimmer who taught me how to make my first cyanotype at Bristol Folk House, and the people and places that prompted these poems.

LAY OUT YOUR UNREST

www.ingramcontent.com/pod-product-compliance
Lightning Source LLC
Chambersburg PA
CBHW040522220526
45473CB00013B/2956